curious about

ICE STORMS

BY DEBORAH SCIGLIANO

AMICUS LEARNING

What are you

curious about?

Curious About is published by
Amicus Learning, an imprint of Amicus
P.O. Box 227, Mankato, MN 56002
www.amicuspublishing.us

Editor: Ana Brauer
Series Designer: Kathleen Petelinsek
Book Designer and Photo Researcher: Sara Hood

Library of Congress Cataloging-in-Publication Data
Names: Scigliano, Deborah A., 1951– author
Title: Curious about ice storms / by Deborah Scigliano.
Description: Mankato, MN : Amicus Learning, an imprint of Amicus, [2026] | Series: Curious about extreme weather | Includes bibliographical references and index. | Audience: Ages 6–9 | Audience: Grades 2–3 | Summary: "What is an ice storm? Learn the causes and effects of one of nature's most slippery and dangerous weather events in this question-and-answer book for elementary-aged readers. Includes infographics, table of contents, glossary, books and websites for further research, and index"— Provided by publisher.
Identifiers: LCCN 2025012817 (print) | LCCN 2025012818 (ebook) | ISBN 9798892008419 library binding | ISBN 9798892009072 paperback | ISBN 9798892009737 ebook
Subjects: LCSH: Ice storms—Juvenile literature
Classification: LCC QC926.37 .S383 2026 (print) | LCC QC926.37 (ebook) | DDC 551.55/6—dc23/eng/20250721
LC record available at https://lccn.loc.gov/2025012817
LC ebook record available at https://lccn.loc.gov/2025012818

Photo Credits: Adobe Stock/ronstik, 10–11; Alamy Stock Photo/Michael Gadomski, cover, 1; Dreamstime, Risto Hunt, 8–9; Getty Images/Ali Majdfar, 2, 7, Bill Oxford, 20, DenisTangneyJr, 2, 12, mujun, 21, NicolasMcComber, 4–5; Shutterstock/ArtBitz, 15, elenabsl, 13, kryzhov, 16–17, Michal Staniewski, 3, 18–19, Yuliia Konakhovska, 21; The Noun Project/Agung Rama, 22, 23, SAM Designs, 22, 23

Every effort has been made to contact copyright holders for material reproduced in this book. Any omissions will be rectified in subsequent printings if notice is given to the publisher.

CHAPTER ONE

What is an ice storm?

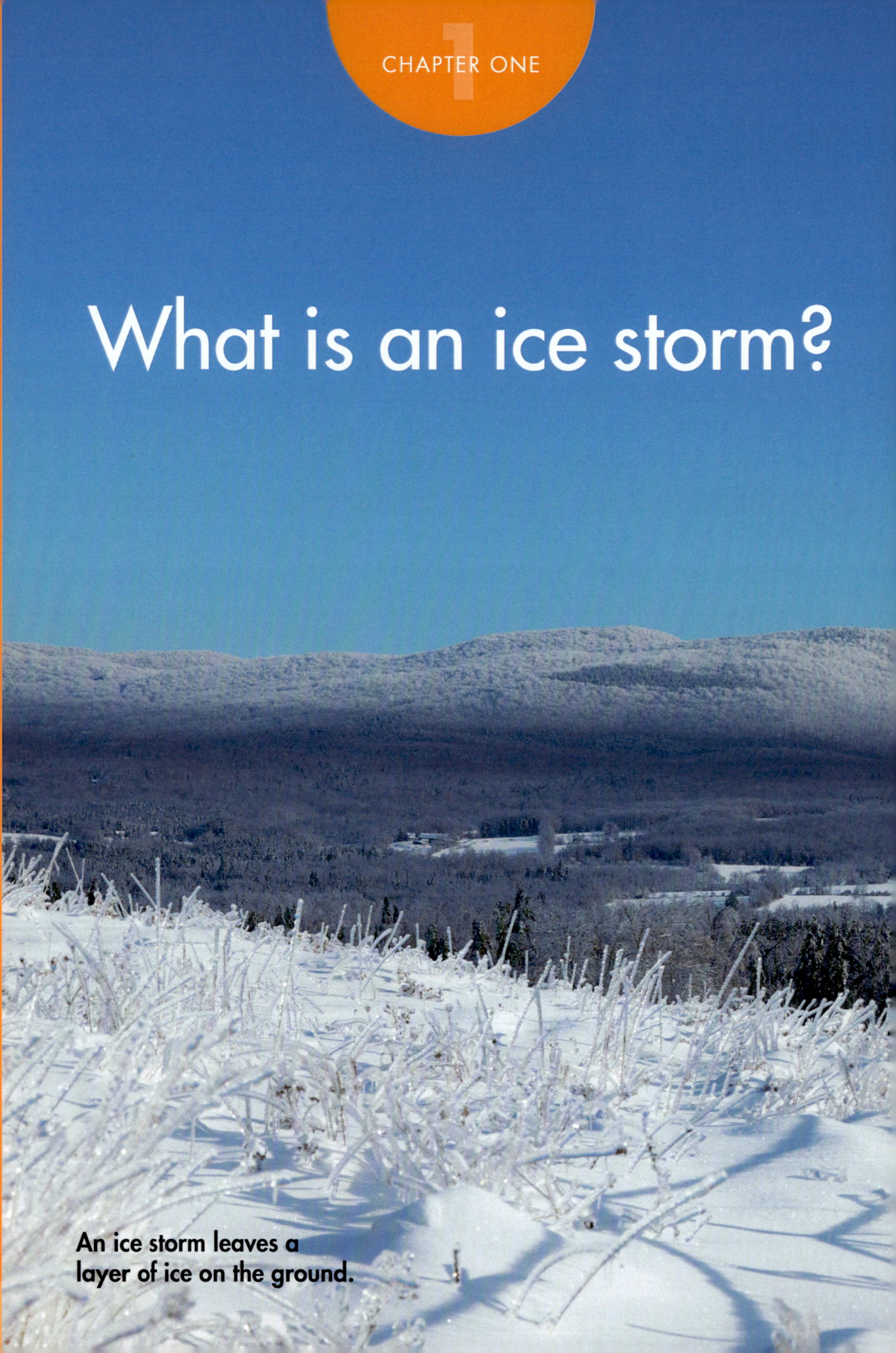

An ice storm leaves a layer of ice on the ground.

An ice storm is caused by freezing rain. Rain falls through warm air. Then it falls through a thin layer of air that is 32 degrees Fahrenheit (0° Celsius) or colder. The rain becomes super-cooled and freezes on contact with cold surfaces. An ice storm has **accumulations** of 0.25 inches (0.6 centimeters) or more of ice.

What happens during an ice storm?

Ice forms on all surfaces. Cars skid on icy roads. It is hard to drive up a hill. It is also hard to walk on ice. People slip and fall on icy sidewalks. Ice covers tree branches. Trees can fall with heavy ice.

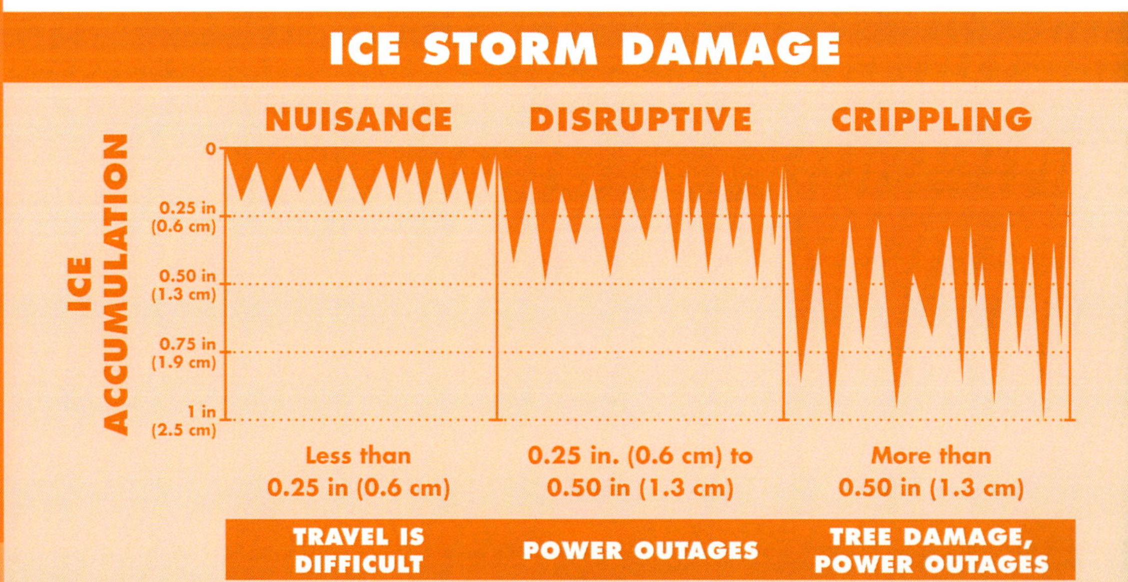

Raindrops from an ice storm freeze into a thin sheet of ice.

DID YOU KNOW?
One of the worst ice storms happened January 5–9, 1998. Places in New York, New England, and Canada got up to 4 inches (10.2 cm) of ice.

How long does an ice storm last?

This car became coated in ice after a freezing rainstorm.

It can last hours or days. The effects can last days or weeks. Cars might have ice all over them. You might not be able to get into them. Power outages may take days or weeks to fix.

CHAPTER TWO

Can you tell when an ice storm will happen?

Sometimes! They are hard to **forecast**. Small changes in air temperature can make a big difference. **Meteorologists** use **radar** and satellites to forecast ice storms. Ice storm warnings might be given between 16 and 36 hours before the storm. Take ice storm warnings seriously.

Meteorologists use weather stations to track ice storms.

How can we get ready for an ice storm?

Listen to the weather forecast so you know when to prepare.

Ice storms can cause power outages. Have batteries and flashlights ready. Charge phones and computers. A portable generator can be used for power. Have a first aid kit ready. Have plenty of food and water. **Non-perishable** food and food that doesn't need cooking is good.

EMERGENCY KIT RECOMMENDATIONS

Why did our lights go out?

Ice can bring down power lines. This causes power outages. A thick layer of ice on power lines can also cause outages. Ice can make trees fall as well. This can cause outages when trees hit power lines.

DID YOU KNOW?

Ice accumulations of 0.50 in (1.3 cm) can add up to 500 pounds (227 kilograms) of weight to power lines.

Ice weighs down power lines and can make the lights go out.

CHAPTER THREE

Is it safe to go outside?

Yes, it can be safe with precautions. Wear warm clothes and spikes on your boots. But ice storms are a good reason to stay inside. Cozy up in a warm blanket. Enjoy a board game with your family. Remember your pets. Keep them inside on cold and icy days.

Stay inside and keep warm during an ice storm.

Can you always see ice?

DID YOU KNOW?
Black ice is common on bridges. Bridges freeze faster than roads. Cold air flows underneath bridges and cools them.

Not always. Black ice is hard to see. It gets its name because it is the color of pavement. It is dangerous for drivers. The road looks wet. But it is icy. Go slowly on any wet surface in the winter.

Black ice can cause slips, falls, and car crashes.

What happens after an ice storm?

Icicles form when dripping water freezes in cold weather.

There are dangers after an ice storm. Icicles form on roofs. Some get very big. They can fall and hurt people. Cold temperatures can be very dangerous. People can get **hypothermia** or **frostbite**. Keep yourself warm with a heavy coat and gloves.

Many trees get damaged during ice storms.

STAGES OF FROSTBITE

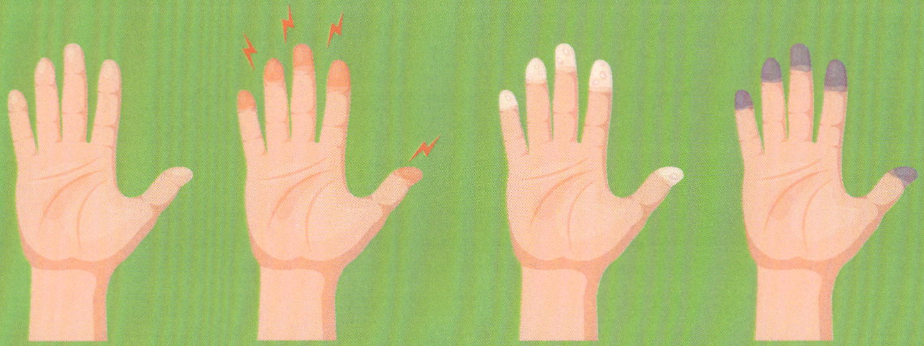

NORMAL

FROSTNIP
Loss of feeling in the skin

SUPERFICIAL FROSTBITE
The skin develops clear blisters.

DEEP FROSTBITE
Joints or muscles may no longer work.

ASK MORE QUESTIONS

What should we have in our car for an ice storm?

How do we keep warm if the power goes out?

Try a BIG QUESTION: How can ice storms be predicted better?

SEARCH FOR ANSWERS

Search the library catalog or the Internet.
A librarian, teacher, or parent can help you.

Using Keywords
Find the looking glass.

Keywords are the most important words in your question.

If you want to know about:

- what to keep in your car, type: CAR WINTER EMERGENCY KIT
- keeping warm, type: KEEPING WARM IN A POWER OUTAGE

FIND GOOD SOURCES

Here are some good, safe sources you can use in your research.
Your librarian can help you find more.

Books

Ice Storms
by Rebecca Pettiford, 2020.

Ice Storms: Causes and Effects
by Anne Winch, 2022.

Internet Sites

Kiddle: Ice Storm Facts for Kids
https://kids.kiddle.co/Ice_storm
Get a closer look at how ice storms form.

Weather Wiz Kids: Winter Storms
https://www.weatherwizkids.com/weather-winter-storms.htm
Learn about different types of winter weather.

Every effort has been made to ensure that these websites are appropriate for children. However, because of the nature of the Internet, it's impossible to guarantee that these sites will remain active indefinitely or that their contents will not be altered.

SHARE AND TAKE ACTION

Create an ice storm library. Collect books that you like to read. Ask your family to collect their favorite books, too.
You will be ready if the power goes out.

Make a roadside ice safety kit. Keep it in your car.
Work with your family to get ready when traveling.

Check on neighbors and relatives during ice storms.
Keep in touch to make sure that they are safe.

GLOSSARY

accumulation The gradual gathering of something.

forecast To predict what will happen in the future.

frostbite A condition in which a person's skin and tissues freezes or almost freezes.

hypothermia A dangerous health condition where the body loses heat faster than it can produce it.

meteorologist A person who studies the weather.

non-perishable Food that does not need to be refrigerated.

radar A device that sends out radio waves for finding the location and speed of a moving object.

INDEX

About the Author

Deborah Scigliano is an educator and a writer. She has taught elementary students and college students. She loves to write for children. Science, especially weather, is a special interest of hers.